WHEN I WAS THE WIND

WHEN I WAS THE WIND
Poems

HANNAH LEE JONES

JUNE ROAD PRESS —— BERWYN, PENNSYLVANIA

Cover art © 2022 by Cody Rex Chamberlain

Author photo: Hannah Lee Jones

Editing and design by Sara June Arnold

Excerpt from *Camera Lucida: Reflections on Photography* by Roland Barthes, translated by Richard Howard. Translation copyright © 1981 by Farrar, Straus & Giroux, Inc. Reprinted by permission of Hill and Wang, a division of Farrar, Straus and Giroux. All rights reserved.

ISBN 978-1-7356783-6-8 (paperback)

Library of Congress Control Number: 2022936657

Published by June Road Press, LLC
P.O. Box 260, Berwyn, PA 19312
juneroadpress.com

First edition: October 2022

Printed in the United States of America

For my parents
who were also the wind

CONTENTS

Several years ago, I stopped submitting my poems to journals and magazines and began posting them to Facebook and Instagram. I paired them with photos of the desert landscape in which I was traveling and enjoyed how the two elements together reflected both a story and state of mind that were evolving and uncertain. I witnessed what I saw, expressed what I felt, and was able to embrace the mess of sharing unpolished work with a generous and forgiving audience.

Only later did I see how all my choices were movements away from what was known, what was tried, into a vast and mysterious territory that excited me. I learned to love it because it gave me permission to more fully express myself rather than following a socially prescribed path that could easily have become the only right way to write or live. What I found is that there is no right way. The way is to wander—not just physically but inwardly—into the wilderness. Jack Gilbert, one of the great wandering poets, knew this wilderness intimately and likened it to a process of "unlearning" the constellations so that the individual stars become visible.

I believe this wilderness exists in all of us.

This book is for you stargazers.

Maps won't tell you anything.

Only the ones you dream about
and wake to find written all over your forearms.

CUMULUS

Desert (Kenosis)

Life, the flight of the alone to the alone. — Plotinus

Before I went out,
I'd heard said in me what was beyond saying.

One day I became the wind:
all sand and memory.

When I struggle to explain this
I point at the yucca flower and scorpionweed.

Or to the cheatgrass and the pale boy lying in it
next to his sister with roots in her arms, her arms his.

A moth roundly gestures toward the truck
they left in flames, a cottonwood coming up
through its smashed-in window.

And finding nothing to touch with its scrutiny,
silence folds itself away like a ledger
in coats of burnished sandstone.

No one will find me on my wrists
and knees beside the night bloomers,
lulled to sleeping by their scent
to be awakened by a sudden bang: their whites unfurling.

When I was the wind
my thirst became clouds,
became rain and sheer rust, wanting
nothing except the sky's changing hands.

Shelter has no words for this. Nobody does.

WEST

azure ✦ sunset, seed of all recall ✦ ether from which all
is formed ✦ soul as mirror ✦ soul as reflection in water
✦ Alice down the rabbit chute, frightened into wonder
✦ oxygen diverted from the seal's heart the deeper it
dives ✦ little deaths daily with every gesture of molt
and shed ✦ the body's sweet harp through which the
blackest days are threaded ✦ truth ✦ the only melody
that haunts ✦ wind ✦ moving nightly over opened
palms ✦ despair's famous brink, so blind it brims with
possibility ✦ desire ✦ discard ✦ how dreams are born

Exodus

Taos, New Mexico

I'd been left.

Dawn found me breathing
some kind of dragon fire,
downed by sycamore smoke
and the final scourings of another night's rain.

Below, the warmth of the village
with its hearths and voices, while I dressed
and undressed myself under the cooling trees.

All of this must be what the ancients knew,
sending their youth into the night
to forage for a dream.

I am the father and mother turning away.

And I am the child
after the horns of the antelope,
her mother and father dead
the moment she leaves the threshold.

Eyes, look your last upon
the things of which you were certain.

The wind and the road are your parents now.
Your new body is happening west of here.

Outside of Hamelin

I was taught to name the constellations.
    As if the stars were not name enough.
As if the girl I was then did not pack
    crates of books to leave, in that season
with its irrevocable music, the solitary
    buck she ran with in woods and fields,
gathering peach blossoms and fireflies.
    As if the fireflies were not light itself,
or the pages they inflamed in the loft
    of the old barn, dismantled by vines.
Tonight I did an inventory: antlers, hooves,
    teeth. Seized the time of our loving
by the forelock and pinned it against the door.
    Where's the wind's key, I kept asking,
that would restore to us our names.
    Something beautiful burned
somewhere, awaiting my return while outside
    the too-small song I'd followed
drowned inside the river.

POINT DEFIANCE

From here you could defy the world, as it were.

Or at least prepare to, wetting your finger
and holding it up to test the wind.

You may think this is neither the time nor the place,
but brother, when I say that war is upon us
I mean our fleets are outnumbered ships to none
and all our notes just a shiver in the distance.

Elsewhere: conjurers would be conjurers.

Beneath their ruses, rumors shaped like the old terrors:
Thermopylae, abandoned compounds
with their cyanide bones.

Did you really believe that if we simply lay still
we could save this place of abalone and its unspent
treasure? We are animals: You
have a perimeter of sound, a perimeter
of vision, listening and seeing only so far.

They will come ashore and make claims on you;
they will tell us this place is not ours,
to be sure you're safe, but of course it is
and you're not.

When the time comes,
let me tell you what will happen:
Your sight will be the first to go.
After that, your hearing.

Never forget the hairs on your neck;
they will know the wind's direction.

When the time comes, as it always does,
stay with me.

ERLKING AT BURLEY'S FIELD

In the field's cratered center
sits an abandoned house.

We've pulled ourselves
from the backwaters
to stand in the marshes
watching hawks fly over.

See the vole in that one's talons
like the wind's collusion with grief?
It is the girl in the car, crying
there's a demon beside her.

There's nothing there, there's nothing there,
her mother keeps saying,

as a nest in the house
rains fur from the rafters,
a gutted mattress slides from its frame,
and what remains of a window
creaks its dirge on a bent nail.

When she curses all sun and rain,
when she blackens their praises
in arsons of young leaves,
when the rivers hoard her hair
and trace the leap and letter of her body,

we will hold her,
we the pierced eye of every storm
and every sin
and every lantern hung inside
her most bitter dream,

we of the lost Ones, holding her now

as she cries *Don't you see, Mother*
and a fox cuts the thicket
with a sparrow in its mouth.

Avian

Spokane, Washington

In a desert city tavern your lips are dry
from kissing the wrist of every woman
who touches your face, unaware it isn't you they want
but the wind's knees, a cloud's hand.
Stormed. Sold-out rooms begging for one more song,
so you play on down the hurricane tracks
to a crowd hushed past the cellar stair
as the key changer suddenly slips from your guitar.

Who do they think I am?

Though once, in autumn, you drew a stone
from a creek and swore that it held tides like the sea,
sang all your songs in a skeleton key
just to remember you have talons and a beak. Fly on,
wings untangling from this psalm of wires, dreaming

Just fly this coop to those cooler nights

Just live that season with its breeze-filled knowing

Just touch and leave this ground with all its excuses

as if you're the only lit payphone in a deserted lot
and you're picking it up, and answering yourself,
and lifting off again over that crush of voices —
then you're gone, beloved only of that falconer no one sees,
no more than a secret stirring in the windbreak's ear.

DEATH WISH WITH LIFELINE

We used to choke each other.
Listen wide-eyed to the heart's tempo
quickening to the edges of what we could bear,
signal mercy and then switch places, give the other
person a chance to see the shadows of the oaks blurring.
It was one of those childhood pastimes that blew off
all sense, like a rogue wind gusting you over
the cliff where you've been teetering,
and on the brink you say *yes.* Yes to more
filth and stardust, just for a second,
amid sunken promises to our adult selves
to stay wild — whatever that's supposed to mean.
I had to get my brother out of bed today.
He doesn't want to live. We rode our bikes
and I watched him hurl his flat-out roulette
down a steep hill, and though he didn't crash
something crashes in me now: the ocean's
breakage in your shallowest breath
calling you back to itself, back to itself.

CEREMONIAL

Gila, New Mexico

Whatever happens with us
already I can see your shadow will stalk these lines,
steadfast as unbent trees rising
from hills newly touched by rain.

Ours would be haunting of the kind
from which one never recovers,
and how do I know this
when all that is touching in this moment are our voices?

Did you know that shamans on the Mongolian steppes
consecrate themselves by burning
pieces of juniper in their mouths?

Imagine the smoke, the movement of palms and knees,
fingers falling away like apple blooms
for that trembling parched kiss.

I was always less interested in recovery
than that holy heat on my tongue.

Whatever happens with us, we will not be far —
with or without voices, pulling each other back
to where the earth awakens us with its stark essence.

ASIN

Demoness of Oregonian Alsea lore

No children for her, or a husband,
or even friends, they were all too unbearable.
She had to be free so she fled,
drank water from wells in the blaze before dusk,
ate roadkill raw, their gore on her face,
wrestled bears in the night, tore through tall meadows
after bolts of lightning. She made love
to lone fishermen and abandoned them, weeping;
stole children and hid them in empty fox dens
to banish them homeward with berries and nightmares,
lawless as ravens and ragged as weeds.
All this she did as she howled and ran;
when the wind changed key, it was her;
it was her when the clouds
wept their storms into buds in spring.
And surely she was the one who shook
your bedroom window to near-breaking,
when you said *I want something but I don't know what it is,*
                                    and so had nothing.

STADELHEIM

Whatever they wanted,
I gave them the name of a child
I did not pray for.

What I would do again:
save her a finger of bread,
steal aspirin from the medicine cabinet,

hide her during inspections
as she swallows against my chest.
What I never once admitted:

the shadow of her behind me —
here, four-footed and scenting my pillow,
there, barely aloft on a column of air

like a hurt hawk returning
in search of her killer.
And what I wouldn't give,

a thousand times over,
to unspill the oil that anointed her
when I walked her to the gallows,

her god shaking the walls of my cell,
for the wage of my sin
is the frost of her voice in my sleep.

Vocabulary (Solstice)

Henderson, Nevada

Dusk over a split field.

The moon not yet risen
over your bone-white table,
set for a feast with friends who aren't here.

Just the ghost of the city you left
to find your breath in water,
the fractured soil that suggests
something swam here once.

Your friends would understand this,
night-climbing with headlamps
or passing a six-pack around a fire —

how between you
and what everyone else calls home
a ribbon of asphalt is the line you keep.

Home, we say,
what is it exactly,
as the evening strips bare in the dying light.

Love, we agree.
It grows dark out here quickly.
What a flock of scattered birds we are.

Scattered, but birds. It grows dark.

北
NORTH

sapphire ✦ silence after the word is heard ✦ words
✦ icing night air to shatter at one's feet in meaning
✦ when right, holding out ✦ where right, hanging
on ✦ the heart's kept fire in the inevitable quiet ✦ not
growing up; maturity ✦ nights cloaked over the dead
and unborn, waiting ✦ dark day blacked with cold,
sick yet fertile as the womb ✦ soul as shadow ✦ love's
thorned initiations for the still-born living ✦ soul as
breath in fog ✦ hearth and its still-warm grounds for
loving ✦ dream ✦ out of mind, that place of gesture and
dark birth ✦ death ✦ the sleep of trust that awakens

Underworld

I had a dream of freezing rain.

Midsummer and suddenly I was inscrutable
as earth under eclipse,
all the thrushes in the grass gone quiet.

And daily the motor of urgency
in that quiet, every blossom or fruit
washing out to that numbness.

You're subjected as always to the same consolations,
Count your blessings
or *You're stronger than you think*

when like a vessel
you drown going into yourself
and strength requires all the not-thinking you have left.

I could say the not-thinking
manifested a new dream; it didn't.

I could say the tossed vessel
held me; it wouldn't.

I had a dream of freezing rain,
adamantine in its brightness.

And in that freezing brightness
I'd made a home that was never a home.

Caduceus

The heart's eyes know.

The breath of you in my hair
before you even entered the room.

Still I marked how you moved,
a wind's tracery over tire tracks,
you inside me later like a fox through an alleyway.

Or an indwelling of moss,
blueprinted as if for always:

you were the flammable face of the world,
in love with a cave painter
who dealt only in echoes, all water.

Their time together sweet
but not without its knives,
their parting: blackness.

There's a halting that's befallen me.
It's set up shop in my body,

so where to place my hands
except this trench between seasons?
Its twofold winding. Its singular scar.

Sometimes I feel it as a fist carving syllables,
as separate from you as the light is
from what it shines upon.

But I'll never refuse your face at sunup.
I can't say anything to you except in tongues.

Ellipse in Wartime

A mayfly born
in the morning
on a long summer's day
knows nothing of darkness.

     In an island labor camp
     men and women carry stones
     from a quarry. Their breathing
     stills the air's emptiness like a hand.

Somewhere a hospital
fills with the dying.
Food trays are left outside
the doors. Lovers

     get in bed with the ill
     despite their fear.
     Elsewhere a revolution
     in which a soldier sees an enemy fall

and helps her up.
Back on the island
a stone is dropped;
there's an execution

     by gunfire while even the owls
     in the trees cover their eyes.
     What can we ever know of grace
     except the blind joy of being spared?

Back the stone
rolls again to the blood
of eastern forests at first light.
Having lived, and only lived,

the mayfly dies at four
in the afternoon.
It will never know
the meaning of *night*.

Mortal Remains

Point of Pines, Arizona

They didn't want to live here anymore.
And didn't want anyone else to, either.
Things Esau must have burned:
pottery, corn husks, relics worn
at each taking of a maiden's hair.
Perhaps after the sun blazed from the chaos
there was Cortes's gold, turquoise, baskets
to hold what they couldn't carry,
scaffoldings falling away to reveal cities
in the sky, glittering white with impending death.
There are thunderclaps in the rubble here.
Perhaps rumors of drought led to killings,
stars drawing javelins in the night
as the people fought, their eyes the black
of extinguished coals. Like the torches
we lit to ignite the rooms we slept in,
saying *I don't want to love you anymore,*
but I don't want anyone else to, either.
The fires gulping the bones of all they had built.
The light that spelled their glory spelling their ruin.

DATURA

Mesa Verde, Colorado

Any trained ear will hear them in the desert's silence.
Voices over the mirage. Unlit fires. Wounds
back-biting what bit them. Fires extinguished, fires
loosed to gallop over distances human and not
human. Figures at dusk bearing the urns of what
never gave, putting down tracks among the shards
of what did. Sirius barking its wild red flash, nights
flooding blue off the silk warm days. Notions. Another
ill-advised stop in a long line of passions. Something
strange that blooms in the night's marrow, bloodless
even while it runs. You may think you will die here;
you may fear to rove in sand until thirst abandons you.
Give me greasewood and blossoms, the diamond
tributary where everyone I've been returns to flood
my future self free. Give me a loom of stars drawn
over my head by a moon so callous that some nights
it almost seems kind. If I should crawl, let me crawl.
If I should fall, I'll be the falling. Just let me live life
at the flood, where everything terrible winks at me
knowingly. Where the ruins are beautiful.

A Marriage

Under heaven thunder rolls: All things attain
the natural state of innocence. — The I Ching

As when once at dawn two dragons duel
       in a meadow, their keepers mad.

       Blood stains their scales black and yellow.
A temple bell rung by the moon's marked climb

hangs like the dead, and a king rises
       from slumber to read his scrolls in the light.

       His queen: the captive scribe who grinds his ink.
Their servants the exploded rays

of every hour they keep their robes.
       How whitely they whisper to each other

       in notes of bitter herbs — their lips bearing
all that's been writ large

or small in the shallows of their skin.
       His eyes adrift like the wind.

       Her fingers weary with language.
Their silences poured along the ground

like so much pine smoke
       while their burning brims over, labors long.

       As when once at dusk I go to a grove
to meet my life's two takers,

and they come to keep their vows,
       and death sends word.

SEVERANCE

So it is with this calamity: it does not touch me ...
                                        — Emerson

He is abandoned in that snow country
after the ice broke and his truck went under,
his words erased with the fuel and cargo,
prey to the madness of a bridge over a floating world.

What errand for a howl with no walls to receive it —
one wind slamming through him, toothless and jawless,
two foxes loping over a blanched desert, his tears
sharpening with the nights. His wife is a prism casting

blank in him as the light wanes, she who made him
long for a house whose beams had not been stolen,
who handed him a scripture of surrender to that cold
and its plow. He moves on all limbs, as if toward

a memory of split wood, the ice beneath him running
to veldt, its margins slashed and burning. There is an eye
in this place that watches none but the invisible, an ear
heeding a voiceless breath that orders him now to go,

to go down into that mistake of salt and untie his shoes.
For this ground is hallowed. For tomorrow the woman
who comes to claim him will find him buried in the drifts
and shadows of that long way, her own silence deepening

with the banked snow, and she will wade with him in her
arms into the marshes of their spent darkness, his one
secret misting from him, and listen for him — long enough
to hear the wolf of him singing, flanks on fire, ashes sown.

END OF THE CONTINENT

When we reached the Pacific it was time to die.
Sandlance plied low waves with scales
so shimmering we could have leapt.
But this was no time for leaping,
the ropes of eelgrass at our ankles.
I said I didn't want to go. You said *We're all*
on the line and I tugged at your sleeve as if to stay
though I had to leave, and to me it all felt the same.
I hoped you would forgive my mistakes as I ducked
into the current. Salt chill seizing my throat. A new day
breaking amber, setting free its new swallows
with hands seagone in their rise and sigh.
I rose and dove in the waves, blue trees of every shape
laddering up from the ocean floor. In an oak's high
branches I stopped to look back and saw
on shore, through rainbows thrown by fishes,
you waving, your own leaping, line after line.

ELEGY WITH OPENED COMPASS

Brewster, Washington

You   who gusted faithfully through forty Junes

as if possessed by a thousand promptings of light

glinting on the steel armor I recast to fit

you   at twelve   twenty   thirty   thirty six

how long did I refuse you   who were

the cold sea's wrath   or the cliff jumper's riven face

lying in red rooms with a needle in your flesh

to lose the repeated stabbings by rain

Now you   you   and you   come with me

row with me through these tides in the grass

rock in my arms beside the laid-down scythe

Let's kneel before this hour with its back-lit slenderness

as I gather you into me   past ones   haunted

saying   go now   rest now   thank you for keeping me safe

After the War

Let's say there's a tomorrow.
To wake in a twist of sheets so soft
all hurt vanishes from the world.

That just perhaps, not a moment
too soon, all my old clocks
with their tarnished hands

will declare peace over both
our cities, burnt to their undersides.
Every streambed praying for a howl

when what I long for is water,
to be seen through that water.
What are we doing?

So much is unknown to me
in these weeks spooling past us,
trackless as a throng of ghosts.

Tell me something real
and I'll draw from your tears
until I've found my strength again.

Show me the feeling of grass,
the helicopters of the dragonflies.
That the light will shine from our recoil.

EAST

SPRING

emerald ✦ drum of sunrises ✦ skeletons risen by a
morning's breaking ✦ eyes knitting anew what's been
sundered by lightning ✦ some small tune voicing
your yearnings, unconfessed ✦ all of the bold heart's
smoldering unrests ✦ sticks of foxfire and the light
they bring ✦ furred or feathered down of every wild
young thing ✦ time ✦ crying joy at lettings of long
rain ✦ time in the river's sharp cracks like a song ✦
Maytide's warm way, how it mouths the dawn ✦ the
writing of what's real, which survives all wrongs

EXILE

Moab, Utah

I have chosen and not chosen this place.
It loves me and is branded to me:

This sand in my eye. This wind
which speaks to me only when I've lost my way,
these rains that come to batter
without satisfying my thirst.

Each day a visitation, the long nights
of animal sleep spooling out to leave
their footprints at the door like departed guests.

I push onward without you.

Some days the storms throw things at me.
Some days I am the storm.

Some nights I am the moth
who thrashes around the room
painting pieces of herself onto the globe of the lamp.

We know that even stones can be born aloft on the wind
to have the ground rise up to meet them in answer.

Tell me there's a place where the past can gather.

Imagine me happy.

When My Mouth First Opened

The known world was in whiteout.

A woman flew over my orchards
with her housecoat in flames.

Skies which had once been given
to every shape of star

darkened for the utterances
I thought would end me.

Instead there was wind.

It pushed me northward on a river
through a thicket of lupine.

The woman over my orchards became
a deer eating snow out of my hand.

Some days a black lightning arrived
to wick the blindness off my body.

Last night I dreamt I was the deer.
Her world felt realer than this one.

And out of it came a singing:
too fine to be that of birds,

too unknowing to be human.

DAUGHTER OF CAIN

As sons and songs go, some precede
      the others like a major chord,

      barbed as they are with the mercies
of an inheritance. The winter I lost my skin

to my cousins in a cedar hollow, my father's spade
      silver in my ear, a wolf's head

      found me in a field of downed
hemlock, took my left hand

when I couldn't reunite it with its body.
      I know it seems like surrender

      that I knelt to its wake.
It would seem like surrender that I gave my right

hand to its cold flame as it swept the meadows
      like a thin hunter.

      It was nothing. Except it was silver.
It steals through my blood when the north wind

returns to claim what I lack, and I kneel once more.
      I kneel once more:

      heaven knows what hell
moved his offering to another war.

Trees stopped crying as they were cut
      and whispered as they fell —

here into the drawn breath
of another morning, once-phantom moons

sprouting from the old stumps like a second coming,
surely a god somewhere.

O god somewhere: find me
in some bramble among the crows, sealed in prayer.

Find me in these woods
where we die and rise again.

THE FOXES

after Franz Marc

Leaving the chill pretenses of slumber,
we stir. We're high in each other's branches,

slicked with the afterglow of last night's
hard freeze. We've even touched our lips

to its cracked skin futured with orange blossoms
and pine oil, defeated its bitter aftermath,

but not today. All morning I will be cruel,
impassable as a mountain scree steeling

itself in blind snow, and you will wait.
King of my nights, tendril that keeps its promise

to dark soil: Who are you? Fling wide the gates,
teach these torn leaves how to be faithful.

Soulscape (Equinox)

Monument Valley, Arizona

You don't understand why
the dream happened as it did.
But in the dream you knew,
dark in its fullest measure
when the sun wasn't nipping
at the shorn legs of the stars.
Last night I became one of them,
my light adding its notes to all
the others, this dust in my body,
because in a dream one
simply grasps these things,
until day again knocks
and the door of night opens.

The Four Seasons

Death Valley, California

It's morning. You say you had a dream
        where I'm asking if you know
        of a hotel called the Four Seasons

and you're excited and you're wondering if
        I got us a room, and mysteriously I say
        Well, why don't you ask me?

Love moving from noon to night to the next
        day, the glens turning color.
        A boy pacing behind bars,

hidden in his smallness with the keys
        inside his pocket while I say
        nothing that isn't mine to say

and a mute wind hurls an oak's shadows
        onto the floor. Who could ever hold
        against the terror of things that change?

You wanted the Four Seasons. Locked
        in spring, we never made it to winter, couldn't
        handle the winter, boy who couldn't ask me.

LETTER

You'd gone mute —

like the doves on the wire,
having sung against the moonlessness
something large that was never us.

All of a spent season
hot enough to scare me sideways,
something between us withering

too deep for surprise.
And after the flung silences, glass breaking.

I suppose this is one way houses burn to the ground:
A girl for whom only land is god,
striking a match inside your halls of cool marble.

Can you bear the light that it throws,
the nights in recoil like whipped dogs,
and touch the not-beautiful inside myself as well as you?

Look at me once without distortion, darling.
Look at me where these high flames taper and run clear.
Hear me out just once in the vault you keep, darling.
Say of what you can see clearly that it was good.

Mountain (Habitus)

The photographer's "second sight" does not
consist in "seeing" but in being there.
— Roland Barthes, *Camera Lucida*

Much as we might strain
ourselves, who has the eyes to see? Not

these shallows with their rests
    and silences cut small by our deafness.

        Thieves in a temple. Even the stooped
ceilings with their copper bells know

what the rain for all its hollows holds
        captive. How shamelessly love persists

    in unmaking itself, becomes
food, the voices multiplying. I am only

spirit where I unthink myself clean,
        the soil in the runoff, here

        with my skin. Here with the feast
table's wood grain, the shutter clicking,

the offerings on the altar:
        fog, peonies, and allspice.

Highlander

Would you know
I'd just been dreaming of us.
All right, I know you said
you dreamt of me first, but the veil
between dreaming and living is thin.
The more so for the moon's red truces
with daybreak, running low.
And would you know
you're more than a diminished night's own,
scarred as we are
in this moment we've been fearing —
the one where you say
through the salt on our tongues
not to live for the promise of silver
in the vault or the carving of the ghosts
of our names into granite.
Just tell me one last time
about the tracks you laid on the railroad,
the grove of ancient walnut
where you divided the beams.
Or the opened doe you found there
with her heart still going.
You know where I've been.
You don't care about that,
asking to see my hands
and hear my new songs,
all the artifacts I've yet to unearth.
Would you know last night I dreamt
you somehow kept finding them,
that it was me instead of you
chasing the hours into the open.
The dirt under our fingernails
lode enough to see by.

STEPPENWOLF

Know thyself? If I knew myself, I'd run away.
— Goethe

And so what if you did. All the hours
       we squander just to see who's watching.
And clear along its axis
       the body, swarming with white lights.
This thing happened, then the other,
       trying to understand how
until nothing could remain
       to possibly start over from.
Because the end of the world will not be hellfire
       but the eons passing over
your hidden face, and under the gentlest rays
       even the grasses must wither.
Is yesterday over yet? Shall we race against
       the birches to see who can let go first?
Here now is the earth. Here now
       is the wind raking over
the coals of gone fires, her hand in your hair,
       your finger on the day's pulse
beneath the one that's on replay.
       If we could only stop:
The old movies staring at us
       from street corners like found thieves.
Soon you'll pay out the old thunders
       that shook you sightless,
but they can wait, because animals
       always know what to do. Emptied
down to nothing, they think of rain.

SOUTH

vermilion ✦ always so emotional ✦ heat ✦ earth's,
and the body's ✦ that other language of the
body, interminably wise ✦ raspberries, sweet-
bitter in the lilt and loam of seasonal densities ✦
midday making much of the nearly nothing
that is left ✦ orgasm's rise and fall, with its
geometries of breath ✦ permission to back out,
and in backing out, dance ✦ the first dance ✦
the last dance, turning already with song into the
next ✦ evening then night then the last day, shining
and dying ✦ life on all burners ✦ remembrance

Where I Lived and What I Lived For

Green River, Utah

To be alone on this red earth
where no one comes to visit me.

To crawl there, the words entering
sidelong where the skies lift open.

To be the night whose songs unsing
themselves in the space opened by just words.

To be equal parts light and darkness.

To be the light whose chains on me
were god once, and shall be again, in darkness.

To be wholly dusk and dawn,
the hours closing with dulled stars
the far distances between.

To become nothing of importance,
for good and forever,
never asking each other what we've made of our lives.

To be springtime, ebbing greenly even as she brightens.

To be the soul on fire, declaring that it's time.

The Answer

Then one day I invited pain
    to take a seat in my house,
        asked it what it wanted,

anything that would shuffle off
    its watch over my nightly turning.
        I said I wanted spring.

To see the skies again
    with their eddies of birds,
        enough so that for once

my thoughts with their acid rain
    could eat the remains
        of what did not last.

To my pleas for leniency
    pain said nothing.
        Instead it knelt beside me,

and in the bruise of that sundown,
    in the heart's tiny vault
        where only dreams can enter,

it quietly said *Look at me*,
    and the moment I looked,
        it left me.

Sunyata

And when the girl asks her why that man
set himself on fire, how is she to respond
except as any mother hemorrhaged by loving would,
that someone so wild for a clear sky would think
to exit famine by way of a lighter and gasoline,
every building and street light kept eyewise on him,
what a price his life was, what miracles are seeds
sown in flames, and what a fearsome wind
his god must ride upon; the only unspoken thing
a fraying of tissue into carbon like a seal engraved
with a dragon's face, as if there were nothing to hold
heavenward in the wake of a monk's beating
or a screamed prayer out of a lit alley
in a dream no one wakes from; and all this
while somewhere in the world another girl asks
her mother about death and her reply comes
more as a question in itself, something
about grace arriving with a phoenix in her hand,
no souls above the wind and no stones
rolled from their graves, only grace herself saying
in the name of my many names, let there be nothing
on earth but this, my hunger, your brightness.

Schoolmaster

The day her mother scried her with owl talons
    to instruct her in a child's black liturgies
you found her eating alone in the library stairwell,
    the sea of her gone to stone.
At first you couldn't see her face blooming
    beneath gauze like the repeated
wreck a lark makes of a mirror.
    Nor could you persuade her to let
the father in you loose lightning on her house,
    to help the helpless meet fire with fire.
So, how it takes you back to see her as a woman,
    arrows on her waist and leaves in her hair,
to blink back to a girl on her knees begging
    you to say nothing, that her mother is good,
while outside the river's respite tripped and ran on.
    But with your arms you scooped her up
and carried her to this place, the carpet she stood on
    bent back to its born shape
like grass after a doe rises from winter.
    Remember in this new freedom how you said
to her *All right*, then gave her a length of chalk
    so she could score this night for singing.

Happy new year of marveling at how different and
alike we are, in a Korean restaurant that's so busy I'm
crammed against an Indian mother who's with a boy
who looks more like me than her. I'm puzzling this out
when she explains that her son is by the counter and
the one beside me is his friend, together for a Lunar
New Year that's two weeks of *bao* and sticky rice and
strangers around tables like ours, a scrim of bamboo
leaves on one end and steaming bowls of *manduguk*
on the other. Our waitress reminds me of my aunt
who just died, the leather-jacketed guy in the corner
is a doppelgänger of my father at twenty, and I'm
pretending this kid with soup glazing his chin is my
little brother. It's hot, he complains. I tell him I hear
him: hot like the wild-eyed horses our ancestors rode
thundering over deserts you and I will never see. Hot
like my father at twenty-two, looking like a Mongolian
John Wayne, but that was in pictures. Now I'm outside
the corner store watching lion dancers wish the owners
a year of good fortune, their golden legs spitfire,
fuse-linked firecrackers in the door burning up all the
Lees, Kwongs, and Changs to the drop-beat of drums.
Baldwin disdained the term "melting pot" because
who wants to melt? My father at twenty-four thought
better, which is why he scaled the steps of my mother's
Manhattan apartment and pounded the door all night
to the rhythm of his loneliness, until she flung it open,
crying *All right, all right! I will marry you.* And so I was
born not of my parents but a welter of syllables, none of
which I remember at the kung fu demonstration where
I spot the little brother of mine, the soup gone from his
face, beaming in the crowd and who could no more be
my brother than that Black boy splitting a cinder block

could be Chinese. Oh me, oh life, here's to another year
of pride in whatever you are under the scarlet lights of a
holiday that is and isn't yours, mouthing verses in a play
where your teacher calls you by the name of your Filipino
classmate, and you feel alike, and different, and lonely, and
no longer lonely all at once.

BOYS

Joshua Tree, California

With their nonstop questions:
I knew them only with my eyes and ears.

All the days long they played
with wind, their only willing companion.

Days of no wind,
days of sun livid enough
to ignite the cookfires they'd burn themselves on.

I heard them scream.
I watched the seamless coup
that was their mother and grandmother.

Boys in the wind,
toted off by their mother
to another precinct fatherless.

I watch them leave.
I hear them cry

and I wish I could tell them,
and the girl I once was,
I'm sorry there was no one to love you
when you were so, so afraid.
I'm sorry no one held you when you were sad.

ORIGIN STORY (REMEMBRANCE)

Genesis. Born of god's eye
                we weren't fish in the sea

but the young light refracted
                we weren't birds in the air

but the waves their new wings
                inscribed on the first dawn.

Look: their rivulets on our ankles
                entrenched as tattoos.

We won't pretend they're not there as weaponry
                like claws

or teeth or venom
                for as any good animal knows

there's a calculus to the way
                a child grows into a brute

who won't stand too close to a mirror
                and the mirror knows us

too well: the tidal in-rush of breath
                the insomniac's red backfill

for even as god said it was good
                a storm will always claim its own

and we were born of the storm, brother.

                The sea is going to come for us.

LONGING TOWN

Wind with no father, and father to no one,
bless my brother who hanged himself from an oak
the summer my song split in two:
the one of me who hid from the blacks of his eyes
and the one of me who wanted nothing more
than to touch them as the fir cones dropped,
as we batted sticks at thistle tops in August
to ignite the fields with their sparks.
He was the boy, you remember, who always wanted
a tail, not so much for balance in falling as the stab
of falling itself: tail over head, head over hands,
until the ground of some town would kiss him.
Any town but our father's. As this one had:
the hemlocks nesting the oak, the oak nesting the boy
and the shredded notes of robins hanging from his fingers
as the sun fell, and you whistled and sang in windows flung
open, the ghosts of gone bucks listening from the porches,
toward a man and the son he touches,
toward a boy who is more than spring,
more even than my brother's laughter white like birches,
toward my boy on his tricycle among men with chainsaws,
men of cordwood breaking ground together,
and bread, their troubles fed to the fires,
the leaves flaming behind him as you bear him away.

FIRST RIDE

after Johannes V. Jensen

And when the stallion threw me again, there arose
with the dust something beyond a mind's apprehension:
Sweat. And muscled in its wake a shyness
so deep it must have risen from his heart's floor,
a dominion so gone even mice would find nothing
in its cracks for forage. How out of such ruin
could a girl make contact, except by a thievery
that murmurs like the fall, *You don't have to do*
anything you don't want to. I was done approaching him
with hand outstretched while throwing a shadow
that held the whip. So instead I took up space
beside him, started acting like another horse:
cleaned stables to a silence so black it was lost on the crows;
went out at first light to watch his muzzle steaming.
You learn that carrots can just be carrots.
That what remains unbroken between woman and beast
is an echo more ancient than Scythian graves
and their linen-wrapped horses, back to when
the words *I'll carry you* first met the words *I'll care for you*
and loved them back; when *I'll carry you*
became the promise of draped arms, lean neck,
of legs around a torso, and we rode out
of the village toward the open steppes
to where the rain always rises. It takes a wild patience.

PRONGHORN

When death came over me
and took my eyes
the ground everywhere shook

Somewhere in the world
the kings were angry
at me, I already knew

So son it's your father
back from the slopes
with the song I found there in the grasses

There was a long dark path
and the light sprang a latch
Then I opened my eyes to the treeline

In the light of November
there you stood
asking if I'd finally see you

Remember how I taught you
to run or be hunted
I kept running and I take it all back

Back to the sedge where
we look at the stars
and I say *I'm glad* and you say *I'm glad*

CHIMERA

When the keepers of fires were all murdered, I fled.
  And the heart became bone.

Heart of that season's woundedness:
  a white apple, glittering
  with the first hard frost.

Once, a stranger came to my bedside in a dream.
  With a blade he split me open
  as one would split an oak.

No pain — just terror at a stone glowing red
  where my heart should have been.

The weariest stone I'd never seen,
  which I learned was the core
  of that season's fruitfulness.

So you tell of a bone-white calling in the distance,
  alive with such sadness
  as to slow the heart.

White and red, both, is what you are when it comes for you:
  You the keeper,
  the fire, the blade, the stone.

Coda

LINEAMENTS

All else is but as a journal
of the winds that blew while we were here.
                                    — Thoreau

I.

And then the day came when I turned,
for a season, into the body's hunger to run.

Not that I was so free
tracing the parabola of each day's sun
toward its extinction
at the ankles of pear trees.

Of the things I took from you
I regretted most the marigolds
on the ridges your eyes make when you're happy,
thrushes flipping leaves after worms.

And then there were my dreams, always at odds
as to whether to feed dead things
to the garden our years together
had left fallow — stripped vines,
the greens and golds going, my hands in your hands.

In the moments then and since
I've had nothing to offer you. Nothing,
perhaps, except a jar of my breathing:

the scent of the tea olive always strongest at dusk,
loud as our silences allowed, saying,
                                    Be here with me.

II.

Still of bottomless night: in the dark,
it isn't the way the mind
unmasks itself that comforts me

but the nightmare galloping through it,
haloed in its going by stars of lit dust.

How fathomlessly she moves,
with no bridle, rolled-back irises
searching the earth for another season's blooming.

Say she's your last prayer
in a tongue no one understands:
all sweat and breakneck, so much so

that you will find her rider kneeling in a field
where a swift has written its bones into the snow.

For now she is all winter.
The scent of her etches you clean.

Only later will you see how her dying was fruit —
fisted buds rupturing green
into a bower of flaming swords.

III.

Eden. If I was to be a harp
played by the world's winds
I was never to reenter.

There my angel keeps watch,
a figure in the shape of what I never lived,
repeating himself in the high notes of eagles —

and though I never became
the falcon or storm or great song,

perhaps it would satisfy him
that I dredged myself from blackened rivers,
pure enough for charm.

Pure enough for what the soul knows,
which is what the waters won't give up
until their secrets are all risen:

a tune in your deafness
the finest strings could only dream about,
the nests they weave,

the knowing that, more than darkness or wings,
we're the night pulling back the night.

IV.

When you come home
be sure it's for the lovers on the river
whose last fires are recorded
in the scrolls of birch woods.

The breezes will no longer matter:

We all look so radiant in the heat
of what we could lose,
on this earth where we know the wildflowers.

Closing your eyes you see them burning,
so faithful and bright
you could believe in death.

We can be afraid, we who in living
choose to bear the scars of what we are,
scraping our keels in the mud of what wants to vanish.

And we can waver, burning onward
with our opening and closing —

the hands of the world will still be touching us,
leading us first one way,
then the other.

LEGEND

I came here knowing everything
I needed to know to survive.

Then I lost it on a swollen cut: the soul's cry
for tenderness, begging for water.

I was casting about
for something to break
when the wind overtook me.

And it held me as I retraced steps
on a stair the years had left sagging,
the long days of signal fires telling me my life.

The wind kept holding me until I became it,
held me and held me
until one day she was gone.

There's this moment when you lose
yourself to the thundering world
to be danced for a change by your own lost music.

The very air around you
bending you back to your origins,
saying *only you, Light. Only you.*

Some readers' experience or impression of poetry is that poems erect walls rather than removing them. In the case of this book, some degree of that opacity may be unavoidable, but with these notes I seek to offer a kind of field guide through the poems' territory, drawing readers into a more felt connection with their imagery and language and ultimately, I hope, with life itself.

This book's introduction references a line in Jack Gilbert's poem "Tear It Down."

"Desert (Kenosis)" gestures toward the first step in any transformative journey: hallowing and emptying oneself to admit the full experience of life with no qualifications.

WEST

Archetypally as well as in the Indigenous medicine wheel, west is the cardinal direction associated with the psyche's descent into the realms of the underworld: a place of dreams, encounters with the unconscious, and the dark night of the soul. It's also associated with fall, a season of death and of letting go.

"Exodus" Youth initiation rites serve as an analogue for the changes that are occasioned by severing ties with all that's familiar: one's village, kinship bonds, the usual sources of safety and security. The known, previous self falls away, replaced by the mystery of the journey ahead.

The speaker of **"Point Defiance"** warns a beloved sibling to be on the watch. A nature preserve in Tacoma, Washington, becomes a scene of foreboding and anticipation of war.

"Outside of Hamelin" Lured by false music from the town of Pied Piper fame, the poem's speaker reflects on what has been lost on that journey and how restoring one's "name" is an act of homecoming to the one life that is truly ours to live.

"Erlking at Burley's Field" In this feminized version of the ancient Germanic tale of the Erl-King or Elf King, a malicious spirit who kidnaps the souls of children, voices take center stage as the darker aspects of the girl's psyche— a force she will have to confront in herself for the rest of her life.

"Avian" is for Gregory Alan Isakov.

"Death Wish with Lifeline" Some childhood play behaviors engage in a level of risk that, in their dances with death, are actually attempts to access a larger sense of being alive. The speaker here meditates on a shared memory with a brother whose adult depression paradoxically evokes that intensified state of living.

"Filth and stardust" is from Georg Trakl's poem "De Profundis" (trans. Will Stone).

"Stadelheim" A psychic split occurs during an experience of trauma. Here the metaphor for that splitting is a prison camp and the lies that traumatized people tell themselves to survive. This self-abandonment and denial leads to the death of an innocent past self that goes on to haunt the present one.

"Vocabulary (Solstice)" Spending the holidays alone in the outdoors at a time when my old ideas of community and belonging and shelter were falling away, I discovered "home" in the unassuming rawness of sand and mountains at the darkest time of year and in the wild nonverbal language of that place.

As the cardinal direction associated with the darkest time of year, north holds the prospect of long sleep and the promise of awakening—that after the freezing and death of winter, spring will come again.

Jungian scholar Thomas Moore describes the soul as an aspect of the human experience that is not meant to be understood. Instead we are to abandon any ideas of achieving self-knowledge or "the good life." **"Underworld"** reaches for an alternative, a life embraced fully in even its fiercest struggle.

"Caduceus" considers the transforming but often debilitating nature of love, its power over the body, love's insistence and persistence, and the feeling that in spite of time's passing, one cannot stop loving the beloved.

Written to confront the limitations of my experience, **"Ellipse in Wartime"** attempts to understand why the lessons of history so often fail to sink in. Wealth, power, and even the capacity for survival are often taken for granted, when they result more from chance than choice.

"Mortal Remains" was inspired by Craig Childs's *House of Rain*. The Anasazi practice of burning their dwellings before abandoning them raised the question: Why would they have done this, and what parallels are to be found in our relationships to place in the present time?

In the desert's extremes of heat and cold, the intense light of day and freezing black of night, the dazzling array of wildlife, the persistent nearness of death, life is "on" at full blast. **"Datura"** expresses the yearning for that fullness.

This poem borrows from Rainer Maria Rilke's Third Elegy, from the *Duino Elegies*. The title is a genus of desert moonflower, a poisonous plant known to bloom only at night.

"A Marriage" Images from dreams, archetypal mythology, and the *I Ching* attempt to renew and make strange our relationship to existence, that wild marriage of opposing forces: light and darkness, life and death.

Born out of a long dark night in the middle of my ten-year marriage, **"Severance"** was my attempt at absolution for unresolved guilt and an expression of the belief that after even the most painful separation or dying off, life moves forward.

An essential part of psychic healing is the embrace and honoring of one's past, and also of one's past selves. If poems can be meant as rituals of such prayer and honoring, **"Elegy with Opened Compass"** would be one.

"After the War" An ecosystem ravaged by war becomes the metaphor for a relationship torn apart by conflict and uncertainty about the future.

EAST

As the cardinal direction associated with spring and rebirth, east correlates with all things and moments in life at the very start of their cycle, and with the points in seasonal change where energies are at their peak, when the light is greatest and life rejoices.

"Exile" was written for Phillip R. Jones.

"Daughter of Cain" Here a woman cries out for divine intervention in her quest for identity and belonging, the story of her wounded father coloring her experience of loss and insufficiency. In a bitter but necessary paradox, her redemption awaits in the "silver," the very thing that wounded her father.

"The Four Seasons" The dreamt luxury of a night in an expensive hotel becomes the proxy for a richer life with four distinct "seasons." The speaker's beloved ultimately clings to what is pleasant and discards the rest, losing the full experience offered by the original dream.

"The Foxes" is for George Knotek and takes its title from artwork of the same name by Franz Marc.

"Letter" is one in a series of breakup poems in which the speaker tries to get in the last word. Even as she implores her beloved to see her clearly, there's an honoring of all that was difficult and beautiful about their connection.

"Mountain (Habitus)" If we regard a poem as a series of images, a photographer's interaction with a subject is not unlike a poem's way of seeing—of being fully present, attending to what is sacred, and witnessing with new eyes the treasures of the everyday that we so easily miss.

Written in the early days of the COVID pandemic, **"Steppenwolf"** gestures toward the healing and life-affirming "inner wilderness" awaiting anyone who's willing to face within themselves whatever's difficult to face.

SOUTH

As the cardinal direction of summer and midday, south correlates with life at its zenith, when energies are at their peak. There's a bittersweetness to the rose just before it fades: all things that grow and bloom must eventually diminish.

"Where I Lived and What I Lived For" The poem's title is after Henry David Thoreau, from *Walden*.

"The Answer" Pain here is personified as a visitor to the speaker's home—home being a life in which suffering, instead of being something to vanquish or resolve, can be greeted as a friend and ally who takes us deeper into ourselves.

"Sunyata" *Sunyata* is a Sanskrit word describing a state of "void" or emptiness in Buddhist meditation.

"Schoolmaster" A teacher's reunion with a former student sends him back in time to be confronted with a moral choice, one that is affirmed by the present joy of seeing her grown and well.

"Year of the Jackrabbit" references Walt Whitman's "Song of Myself": "O Me! O Life!"

"Boys" An encounter with two fatherless boys has the speaker witnessing their suffering as she begins to grasp her own childhood experience of abandonment.

With prelapsarian imagery, **"Origin Story (Remembrance)"** captures the struggle of two siblings to defeat the forces of nature that have both tormented them and shaped their lives.

"Longing Town" draws its title from a song by Duncan Sheik.

Inspired by Johannes V. Jensen's novel *The Long Journey*, **"First Ride"** reimagines mankind's relationship with the domesticated horse as a love affair. What is wild in any animal is also what is wild in us, and what is wild in us is capable of a love devoid of expectation, of total acceptance.

"A wild patience" is a reference to Adrienne Rich.

"Pronghorn" is, in the words of the fine editors at The Good Men Project, "a father's dying wisdom to the son he never really knew."

"Chimera" draws upon the many-headed monsters of Greek myth to honor the notion that one's experience and rendering of life can consist of "parts," each with their voices and clarity.

"Lineaments" The title of this poem suggests geologic features on Earth's surface. Its epigraph is from Thoreau's *Walden*.

ABOUT THE CALLIGRAPHY

In a nod to my family's heritage, I drew Chinese characters to denote each of the four directions that divide the sections of this book, along with single-stroke character "lines" for the opening and closing. These were outlined in pencil, then filled in using a Sumi ink pen to mimic the brush detail found in traditional Asian calligraphy. This was a workaround: I may never have learned the art form from my calligrapher father, but the yearning to express will always find its own way.

ACKNOWLEDGMENTS

Earlier versions of the following poems appeared in these publications:

"Outside of Hamelin," *Radar Poetry*
"Erlking at Burley's Field," *decomP*
"Avian," *Lime Hawk*
"Asin" and "A Marriage," *Yes Poetry*
"Daughter of Cain," *The Boiler*
"When My Mouth First Opened," *Ruminate*
"Sunyata," *Cider Press Review*
"Year of the Jackrabbit," *Apogee*
"Longing Town," Brooklyn Poets
"Pronghorn" and "Severance," The Good Men Project

I wish to thank my writing teachers and mentors over the years: Lorraine Healy, Christine Hemp, Vic Vogler, Laurel Vogel, Laurel Leigh, and Susan Zwinger, as well as Susan Rich and Kelli Russell Agodon of the annual workshop Poets on the Coast.

Thanks also to the poets who supported Primal School to teach me and other non-MFA writers how to write a poem: Patricia Colleen Murphy, Tod Marshall, Keegan Lester, Joseph Fasano, Gary Dop, Jason Koo, Caitlin Doyle, Kelly Weber, Sandra Beasley, Anders Carlson-Wee, Matt Muth, Cortney Lamar Charleston, Lauren Camp, Joanna Valente, Niel Rosenthalis, Phillip B. Williams, Emily K. Michael, Catherine Abbey Hodges, Tomas Q. Morin.

I am grateful to Kim Schnuelle and John Tremain, to Phil Jones, and to Brooklyn Poets, Copper Canyon Press, Red Pine (Bill Porter), Deborah Hammond, Michael

Matovich, Jan Woodruff, Grunewald Guild, Hedgebrook, Inked Voices, Hypatia-in-the-Woods, and the Rensing Center for the learning opportunities and gifts of time and space to write.

Wild gratitude to Sheila Belanger and Anne Hayden for showing me the shape of the journey.

I thank my family and friends throughout the world for believing in me and my poems.

And George, for believing in me.

And extra cheers and bouquets to my editor, Sara Arnold, without whose vision and stewardship this book would not exist.

HANNAH LEE JONES is a poet and nomad whose adventures have taken her all over the desert Southwest in search of Jack Kerouac's "timeless, dear love of everything." Born in Camden, New Jersey, to Korean immigrant parents, she worked in marketing and outreach for higher education and nonprofits before setting out on the road. She runs Primal School, a coaching resource devoted to literature and ideas that promote a life of meaning, and her writing has been published in numerous journals and social media outlets. She currently makes her home in Port Townsend, Washington. Look for her on Instagram and other online platforms @hannahwritten.

JUNE ROAD PRESS is an independent publisher based outside Philadelphia. Founded in 2020, the small press aims to produce books of lasting resonance and literary value—explorations of time and place, journeys of all kinds—that lead readers to new encounters, connections, and discoveries, particularly from first-time authors and emerging writers. Find out more at juneroadpress.com.